REVENGE
OF THE
REDHEAD

a poetry collection by

KRISTINA ADAMS

To all those contained in these pages of poetry.
This is how I recovered from our tragedy.

INTRODUCTION

I've rewritten the introduction for this poetry collection more times than I want to count. I was driven by the desperate urge to over-explain myself and justify my creative decisions.

But that defeats the point of poetry.

Poetry is, and should be, open to interpretation. Especially poems like these that are about experiences and emotions.

Yes, these are my stories, some literally, some metaphorically, but when you read them, they become a part of your story. They become open to your interpretation and reflection. That's where the beauty and strength in poetry lies. It means something different to everyone.

The poetry in these pages contains themes of situationships, friendship breakups, workplace bullying, generational trauma, and suicide (in *Grave Regrets*). If any of those themes are triggers for you, please proceed with caution, pause when you need to, and seek help if you feel you need it.

The final section of this collection is about the opposite of those things. It's about healing. Recovery. Letting go. That was the hardest section to write because letting go is one of the hardest things to do.

And I'm not sure I'm fully there yet, but this collection has helped me more than I ever thought it could. And I hope it helps you too.

- Kristina Adams, 2024

PROLOGUE

THE BROKEN DOLL

I am this way
Because you made me.
You trained me
to da*n*ce
when you pu*ll* my strings
that you used
to con*tr*ol me.

I am this way
Because I'm your do*ll*
Mo*v*ing only with your *p*ermission
Painted smile
Dead eyes that still
somehow
Look alive.

I am this way
Because you *lied* to me.
Ma*n*ipulated me.
Contro*ll*ed me.
Because you'll never understand what it's like
to relive what you did
Every day.

I am this way
Because you bro*k*e me.

SHRINKING

Smaller.
Smaller!
Can they still see you?

Have you contorted yourself
to hide behind whatever you can?
Twisted your mind to convince yourself
You're the problem?

Have you hidden your emotions
in a wooden cabinet
padlocked it shut
and thrown away the key?

Can you make yourself any smaller
so they don't know you're still there?

If They can't see you,
They can't hurt you.

Dummy

You trained me
to be your broken puppet
Opening my mouth
only when you allowed it.

I was your
ventriloquist's dummy
Devoid of emotions
life could only be sunny.

My emotions were toxic
while yours were just fine
Even when they laid into me
all the fucking time.

I'm so tired
of being angry at you
But you ruined my life
And I can't forgive you.

ENOUGH.

I split myself in two
in the hopes of pleasing you
But it doesn't matter what I do
I'll never be good enough
for you.

WE ALMOST WERE

EXPECTATIONS > REALITY

Everyone expected us to be together –
is that why we never were?

In an alternative world, we'd probably be together by now.
You with your scruffy hair, sulking into your guitar.
Me with my poetry and naivety.

Your hazel eyes manipulated me into believing your lies
while
you encouraged my writing but killed the rest of me
as I desperately clung to the idea of you and me...

Except it wasn't really you.

Everyone saw the you that you presented
ignoring what you were doing
to poor little me.
I was your puppy, your mule, your marionette,
with so many feelings left unsaid.

Everyone expected us to be together.
Is that why we never were?

FIRST

I sometimes forget you were my first kiss.
You tasted like cheap alcohol,
Smelled like sweat and booze.

It was late;
You stayed over and
we watched *Back to the Future*.
Then we kissed.

It was just like a scene from one of those teenage romantic
comedies
except there wasn't a second date
or a second kiss.

INEXPERIENCED

I thought you were cute,
reflective, insightful,
So I flirted a little.
You were shocked, I think:
as inexperienced as me.
When we hugged,
it was like hugging a robot.
Your arms didn't know where to go;
your body had forgotten how to move.

After our second date –
where we overshared during coffee –
I didn't know what was supposed to happen next, so
I slammed the door.

You stopped coming over to watch *Supernatural*
and giving me your robot hugs
and it wasn't until I stopped seeing you around
that I realised the damage I'd done.

You and Me

Sometimes
I miss you and
Your never ending optimism
Your jolly face
And the way you looked at me.

Sometimes
I miss our catch ups over coffee
Where you'd try to play down how many women you'd slept
with
as if I'd think less of you for it.

But then I remember we were never really friends
We were always something more that couldn't be
because of fear,
because of pride,
because of conflicting futures.

We could never be
because we were you and me.

CHANCES

I gave you chances you didn't deserve
Almost like I wanted to get hurt.
I challenged you and you'd blame me,
It could never be your fault, one day I'd see
How perfect you were, just like everyone else.
You knew that would never happen, though;
I couldn't separate my heart from my head,
My writer from my friend,
So I dissected you, trait by trait.
You stretched your arms and I was six feet away.
I begged you to let me stay.
But it could never end that way.

CUT ME OUT

I miss you.
There.
I said it.
Why won't you speak to me?
Does your cowardice
really hurt that much?
Are you really
jealous enough
to cut me out?
Do you really regret
what didn't happen
enough
to cut me out?

FEAR

You wanted me
But you didn't
You did
But you couldn't.
You wouldn't.

Fucking Cock

You're so fucking cocksure
I'm all you want and more
I'm smart
I'm pretty
I'm so fucking perfect

then why is it me
you constantly reject?

I'm not a dummy
I have a spine
And it's no longer sure
it wants to call you mine.

You open your mouth
I hear bullshit
Please close it again
You stupid prick.

Tell me it's over
Or remember I'm here
'cause if you don't
it will all become clear.

There's enough going on
Don't act like I'm wrong
Grow some balls
and stop making me feel small.

STAY

all i wanted was for the pain to go away
i didn't realise that meant you wouldn't stay
it was too late when i realised i'd fucked up
all the effort i'd put in wasn't enough
to escape the demons that chase me
that block everything i want to see
i just wanted to be happy
i didn't realise that was you and me
until it was too late
you were too irate
to give me another chance
at turning this romance
into something more
something we could endure
something that would last a lifetime
be more than a lifeline
be my reason for everything
my prop to hold me up
when i'm ready to fall down
but i fell too hard
too fast
and now our romance
will never last.

YOU KNOW WHO WE WEREN'T

Sweet Sixteen

My boyfriend cheated on me when I was sweet sixteen
I didn't get it at the time, how he could be so mean.
She had flaxen hair and looked like a doll
and when she opened her mouth she was very droll
but that didn't bother him; she was up for it,
so they went to the park and she showed him a tit
and I'm sure you can guess the next bit.

I only found out because I sent him a text
He didn't reply so I tried to ring
and she answered, practically singing,
'Sorry love, he's moved on!
Said you weren't enough of a woman!'
What that meant I'll never know
I couldn't face him – the words were too much of a blow.
So I went into school, asked the lads to have a go,
But they didn't want seconds, someone else's used goods
They liked the idea of a woman's first blood.

The dirty hypocrites, I'd had enough of it,
So when it was time for PE, I got revenge on the gits.
I crept into the changing rooms and burnt all their clothes
to give them some of humiliation of their own.

(NOT) GOOD ENOUGH

I try to be good enough for you
but it doesn't matter what I do
I rip myself apart
to offer you my heart
but you don't want it
because despite all that effort
I'm still
not
good enough.

SECOND RATE ROMANCES

If I could see you one last time
I'd punish you for your crime.
You tore me to pieces,
You ripped me apart,
You made me feel like I wasn't worth
a place in your heart.

You took me for granted,
thought I'd always be there,
but why did I bother,
when you didn't even care?

I gave you my heart,
you tore it up
And rendered it worthless.

But why waste my energy
thinking about you
when you've probably already
forgotten me?

Why waste my time
on the memory of you
Blaming myself
when the problem was you?

If I could see you one last time,
I wouldn't bother punishing you
for your crime.

Revenge of the Redhead

You wouldn't be worth it
for what you did to me.

I won't waste any more chances
clinging on to second rate romances.
I've learnt my lesson,
I know what went wrong,
but really,
I should've known all along.

TRANSPARENT

I challenged you and you'd blame me.
It could never be your fault – one day I'd see
how perfect you were, just like everyone else,
Except that wasn't me – I wanted to be myself.
I had no idea how to think like your other friends.
To me, you'd always be transparent, afraid;
Too scared to open the gate.
That was too much for you, so you pushed me out.
Just close enough to keep me around
but too far for anything to happen.
So I decided it was time, I had to be strong,
I gave up, I moved on,
but a part of me will always think
You've won.

DIRTY HYPOCRITE

You're a liar, you're a bitch,
You're a dirty hypocrite;
You're a fake, you're a fraud,
Did we mean anything at all?

You bitch and you moan,
You feel so alone,
but you're happy in your solace,
with a heart filled with malice.

NOT A PERSON

The way you put your arms around my neck gave me
goosebumps
But now I think
What a cock.
You poked me in the side because you didn't know what to
say
but online, we'd talk for hours.
You'd look at me with curiosity and fascination
But never love or admiration.
You saw me as a flirtation
Not a partner.
A possession
Not a person.
A plaything
Not an equal.

I thought you were dangerous
But I've realised you were frivolous
Because you didn't feel
You wasted too much energy suppressing
what was Real.

LIES

You didn't want to hear it
But I said it anyway
I put our friendship at risk
Because I hated to see you hurt
To see you lie to yourself
About the cause of that pain
And fester in your denial
About his manners
His charm
His intelligence.
He faked them all
Drawing you in with his lies

WHO ARE YOU?

Boyfriend so threatened
He doesn't recall you
Please go away.

Forget Me

Your love meant as much to me as leaves to a tree
but now I can't remember the blue of your eyes,
the smell of your cologne, or the sound of your voice.
The worst part is I didn't have a choice in any of it:
you shut me out and didn't give me a say.
I tried, I tried so many times to reach out to you,
but the door was locked and I didn't have a key.
For whatever reason, you chose to forget me.

COFFEE SHOP

I always think I'll see you
when I go for coffee.
It was our place
our saving grace
the place where
we were ourselves.
No cliques or classmates or bitches
putting us into boxes
telling us we can't be friends.

It was our place.
And it will always remind me
of you.

ENDINGS

I thought we'd be friends until the day we died
And I'd stay up late that night and cry
But now we don't speak.

There was a leak in our friendship
that turned into a waterfall
Creating a chasm that no words can repair.

I don't know what triggered it
but it's been building for years
and I feel guilty because I've not shed a tear

even though I've lost you –
the person I told my darkest secrets to –
when I thought we'd be friends forever.

What does that say?
Was our friendship always destined to end this way?

WHAT DID WE BECOME?

In My Nightmares

Why do you always come to me
in my nightmares?
As if things aren't bad enough
I have to see your face again:
Round, hazel-eyes; Roman nose.
I only think of you when things are bad,
When I'm angry or when I'm sad,
And in those times I wonder 'what if?'
What if?
What if...

ALL AT SEA

You think you're so smooth you make silk look tough,
But really when you talk, you're sandpaper rough.
Your mind is so narrow you'd fit on a canal,
You think you're a maverick but you sound so banal.
You try to dictate to me how I should be,
but your pitiful attempts leave you all at sea.

I give you a chance to redeem yourself,
but I might as well lecture you on material wealth,
For all you care about is your computer screen,
And yet I'm the one who's being mean.

You need to be taught a lesson in words,
You need to learn to listen to girls,
You need to wake up and stop dictating to me,
Or else I'm going to leave you
All at sea.

STOP CURSING

We're different
yet the same.
This is life
not a game.
Words hurt
when they're curt.
Things change.
Never the same.
People change.
Sometimes.
I hate this.
I don't know why.
I'm too weak
to try.
One's wrong,
but so's the other.
Why can't they bond
over the love of another?

Piggy,
meet middle.
Can you solve
the riddle?
Make things work
Or give up
and return
to the curse.
Maybe you should.
Maybe not.

Revenge of the Redhead

Why are they acting
like such tots?

I'm hurting
from their wording.
So are they.
So stop cursing.

LOVE FADES

People fade in and out of your life
like colours in a rainbow
When you're not ready to say goodbye
they move into another colour
leaving you behind

HE LOVES YOU NOT

He loves you,
He loves you not.
But you won't let him go
'cause he's all that you've got.

He plays you up,
He screws you around,
But you take it every time
like a loyal little hound.

You know it's wrong
but you tell yourself it's right,
You hope that one day,
with all your might,
He'll be the guy you go to sleep with
at night.

But deep down you know,
You really, really know,
that he's crossed the line,
that you've had enough,
And it's time for you
to go.

DIVORCE

Yellow primroses peek through weeds.
A neatly mowed lawn dies.
Fine China plates caked in dried-on roast dinner.
A double bed slept in by one.

FRIENDSHIP: INCOMPATIBLE

I'm really not sure we're compatible anymore,
I mean, what do we have in common?
That we write?
Yeah, I'm a poet and you sucked the life out of one.

INVISIBLE STRING

Where were you when I needed you?
Every time I fell apart it was like
I meant nothing to you.

You cut the invisible string that tied me to you
But you didn't tell me
So I was stranded.

DOUBT

I wish I could say I was surprised
that you didn't show up again
but I've come to expect so little from you
that I double booked myself

knowing I wouldn't really be
double booked.
What does that say about our friendship?
That I expect you to cancel
And you do.

Every time?

What does it say about all the bitching you did
When you now prefer their company
to mine?

ROCKING CHAIRS

You said we'd be old ladies in our rocking chairs
But how can we be when you were never there?
Friendship is more than just fair weather
I want a friend who's here forever
not someone who's in love with spring
but can't handle the bad weather winter brings.

You left the rocking chair beside me empty
When you decided you'd had enough of me
But you were 'just' a friend.
And no one talks about how when friendship ends
it hurts just as much, if not more
sitting beside that open door.

IT SUCKED THE LIFE FROM ME

SUBTLE

You fed my insecurities
Made me believe
they were good for me
A toxic cocktail
I couldn't tell
was poisoning me

EMOTIONAL TRAUMA

I need you to know
that everything hurts
because of you.
I need you to know
Everything hurts
because of what you didn't do.
I need you to know
I'm so fatigued
because you never protected me.
I need you to know
I'm so fatigued
because my body shuts down to protect me.
I need you to know
My muscles tense
because I was so alone.
I need you to know
My muscles tense
because you Failed Me.

BAD TEACHER

How different could my life have been
If you hadn't taught me
that I wasn't good enough?

How much more confident could I have been
If you hadn't said
I didn't try hard enough?

How would my life have been different
If you hadn't humiliated me
in a room full of peers?

I was young, I was scared,
but I shouldn't have been scared of You.

I was sensitive, I was impressionable,
but I shouldn't have listened
To You.

Unanswered Question

How different would my life be
If you'd given me my first yes
If you'd answered my phone call
and told me I'd passed the test?
Would I still be working there now
fulfilling the writer cliche
of the coffee shop working 'amateur'
still finding out who I want to be?

KICK ME

You kicked me
When I was on the floor
You made me
Feel like nothing more
Than worthless.
I couldn't work
Not because of excess
But because your mood swings
Caused me so much stress:
I didn't know
What I was walking into
You were so unpredictable
You didn't care
How you made me feel.

TENSION

If tension were an object
You could cut it with a spoon,
Things are getting really bad
We want him out of this room.

If tension were a person
It would be rather large
with messy hair and a love of fast food
and it would be just like you –
completely rude.

If tension could speak,
Its voice would be weak,
It wouldn't know how to cope,
It would just sit there and mope.

If tension could see
It would see you and me,
It would revel in the mess
and create even more stress.

ATMOSPHERE

Hostility.
A radio station that debates the relevance of the Holocaust
and if people with mental illnesses are making them up.

Trust.
You send dogs hunting for us if we're gone too long.
How dare we leave our desks!

Cold.
Zero degrees outside.
Inside: fan on, window open.
Skin suffocating from so many synthetic layers.

MARVEL

You manipulate people like Kingpin
You think yours is the only way, and that you'll win
Well sorry to be the one to tell you but I'm your Daredevil
And I'm here to put you back down a level
Or two or three or whatever you need
Until those around you are finally freed
From your greed, your control, your manipulation
But it's going to take all my patience
to train up so that I can bring you down
So that when I do, you won't see me coming around
I'll be too smart, too fast, too superhero
And until I've won you won't even know
It was me who destroyed you
Me all along who was out to get you
while you thought you controlled me
And no one could see
But one day, we'll finally be free.

SEXISM

You'll listen to a man not a woman but can't say why
And you can't stand to hear her swear beyond 'my oh my'.
You don't mind if she's out of the kitchen
But she still shouldn't be any richer
than you.

It's unattractive to be competitive and not to dress feminine,
to talk about sex or worry our pretty little heads
about something other than make-up.

We shouldn't get angry because that's not pretty either.
We won't get the job if we stand our ground. Just fired
instead.

LITTLE GIRLS CAN'T HAVE AMBITION

You can't be an entrepreneur
You shouldn't aim so high
Expect less and you'll always be happy
And have just enough to get by.

It's unattractive to want money
And being attractive is important
So earn what you need and nothing more
And your love life won't be dormant.

Pick a job that doesn't pay well
Extra points if you hate it.
Because no female loves her job
Her social life should compensate for it.

Never ask for a pay rise
It's simply unbecoming
You'll never get it anyway
So why chance a reckoning?

Little girls can't have ambition
Because they'll only get hurt
But what the world keeps forgetting
is that you're underestimating our little girls.

GRAVE REGRETS

We stood at the graveside, surrounded by poplar trees.
'I'm sorry I wasn't there more,' you said. 'I was a bad friend.'
I nodded, not knowing what to say as I watched you cry.
'I should've done more. I should've been there more.'
I bit my lip, studying the next grave, which was covered in
an overgrown, forgotten succulent plant.
'Why didn't you tell me? Why didn't I see?'
'Because you didn't want to. You made it all about you.'
You looked to your right, the tears in your eyes alight.
I studied you, wondering if you'd ever have a clue.
'Was I a bad friend? Was that why you ended it?'
'You ignored me. Repeatedly. Your heart turned to stone.
You left me alone.'
*You wiped at your eyes with the back of your fist, singing birds masking
the sounds of your cries.*
My voice cracked as I asked: 'Do you get it? Do you see it?'
You didn't respond. Did you really care that I was gone?
I shook my head. Of course you didn't get what I'd said.
'If I could turn back time, I'd pay more attention. Promise.'
I chuckled. 'No, you wouldn't.'
*After wiping your eyes again, you turned in my direction. You looked
right through me.*

Kristina Adams

RECOVERY OF THE REDHEAD

COMING TO TERMS WITH MY ANGER

I could sit here and be angry
about why I'm filled with rage
or I could sit here and be angry
at how much I lost from such a young age

But holding on to anger is tiring
And I'm already fucking exhausted.

MINDFUCK

The longer I bottle this up
The more it hurts my insides
My muscles get tighter; my heart races faster;
Depression pulls me in and anxiety takes over
I have to find a way to let go
So that I can live the life I want

But it's not that simple.

There is no end to processing the past
It's their problems that destroy my future
So I have to take steps to take control
While letting go of what I can't.
It's a mindfuck
to get unstuck.

CHAPTERS

You took my voice away when I was too young to
understand it
I became too afraid to verbalise my emotions
So I internalised everything, turning my feelings into poetry
and stories.

I can keep rewriting this chapter to see how it ends
but the truth is I'm still stuck in it.
So it's not an ending it's just another scene
another twist in the story I didn't see coming.

I think I'm ready to move on
but this chapter keeps growing
keeps twisting and turning and churning
it's been going on so long it's getting concerning
but how do I know
when it's time to end
the chapter?

SPARK

I won't be forced into your little box
No matter how neat and tidy you like it
I'm not a contortionist and your constraints hurt
They're brutal and unnecessary, as are your words
that suppress me and others like me.
We don't all want to live the life you desire
Some of us dance around a different fire
Don't kill our sparks or suffocate us
Because you're scared of being different.
I'm not hurting you by ignoring your rules.
You're hurting yourself by confining yourself to such
narrow pools.

STYLE

I used to fantasise about a boy whose hair fell over his eyes
I was the only one who could see through his disguise
And I was ok with that.

But then I met you and didn't know what to do
Because you didn't have floppy hair
And you treated everyone fair
There was no facade to see through
You were happy being you
And for me that was totally new.

SOMEONE

I thought I was done
writing about you
but here I am:
writing again.

I'd forgotten you
but you crept back,
and now I'm here
feeling like a rat.

Thinking of you
makes me sick –
you really hurt me
you conceited prick.

The time I wasted
on you is a shame –
I could've spent it
not feeling lame.

It took some time,
but I found Someone better,
Someone kind,
Someone charming,
Someone who's all mine.

Someone who's not ashamed,
pathetic or afraid,
Someone who's so different to you.

A stranger would never have a clue
that I could like such a narcissist
with a heart of stone and who took the piss
behind my back
who was the rabbit to my greyhound track
who broke me down and tore me apart
who covered me in mental scars
and gave up
before things could begin
and left us
in the situations we're in.

What You Missed Out On

I never could let go
of every word that you said so
I'm taking the time to say I'm sorry
for every word that you fooled me
with every lie that you told me
and every time that you broke me
down.

Thought we had something special,
but it was just something tragical
and now I'm here to say I'm sorry
For every lie that you told me,
and how I always would forgive you,
when I should've found someone
New.

But now I'm moving on,
I think I've found The One,
and you're the one who missed out,
'Cause I'm something to shout about,
but I guess you'll never know
how I believed every lie you told me.
Now I know it's not my fault
that you treated me so cold,
you didn't deserve me.
And now you'll never get to see
what you missed out on.

I know it's your fault,
but now I'm so bold
I've moved away from you.
Now I'm someone new.
And I'm the one who's winning
while your head is still spinning.

Take your time to say 'I'm sorry'
that you never did want me
but it doesn't matter anymore,
You're the other side of the door
I wish you had been before.

But now I'm moving on,
I think I've found The One,
and you're the one who missed out
'Cause I'm something to shout about.
But I guess you'll never know
how I believed every lie you told me.

Now I know it's not my fault
that you treated me so cold,
you just didn't deserve me.
And now you'll never get to see
What you missed out on.

UNLIMITED

I thought love was a limited resource
Something I had to keep precious
But it turns out love is infinite.
I had to protect it
Because I was sharing it
with the wrong people.
People who didn't appreciate
the heart I had inside of me
And who only really cared
about what I could do for them.

SOULMATE

I don't believe in soulmates
but if I did I'd know you're mine.
Your blue eyes see right through me
to another place and time.

It's like we've been us forever,
even though it's just fifteen years.
Your strength is what keeps me going,
helps me fight through all my fears.

My life isn't right without you,
I wouldn't know who to be,
but with you by my side I know
I can be anyone I want to be.

BAGGAGE

You carry an invisible weight
and think you're all alone
but that weight's been passed down
through the actions you condone.

The luggage weighs more
with each passing generation
Dragging everyone down
and destroying any chance of a healthy foundation.

The suitcase may be invincible
But the damage can be repaired
Its weight can be lessened
After accepting inevitable despair.

Repairs don't come easy
and they sure don't come cheap
but what other option is there
than emotionally diving deep?

You could sit and you could fester
hate yourself more every day
take it out on everyone around you
until they don't know what to say.

But what good does anger do?
What purpose does it solve?
A life filled with anger
is one lacking in resolve.

TRAGEDY

They met at nursery when they were tiny
Matching mousy hair, their love of family.
Drifted apart as time went on
but always floating back as the years carried on.

Distance gave them the chance to grow,
to meet as teenagers as if they'd never known
each other as kids, all tiny and snotty,
asking the teacher if they could go potty.

Her hair was red now, her temper as fiery.
His eyes were muddy, his body all lanky.
Mismatched, but somehow meant to be
together – a future everyone could see.

They'd end up together; everyone had no doubt –
People reminded them of such, every time they hung out.
It was tedious and embarrassing, but what could they do?
Especially when they thought it was true, too.

They texted and typed, showed affection in emojis,
reinforced their affection, but at a distance that was lonely.
They were cat and mouse, sometimes switching roles
Leaving other friends with the job to console.

He said he loved her, but she'd never be good enough.
He said popularity mattered; her lack of it was tough.
Her heart was broken, shattered into pieces.
The two of them stopped speaking, their fragile hearts
grieving.

Her heart hardened so no one else could get in,
she was so scared of it shattering again.
But one day she met a guy, kind with blue eyes,
And she couldn't stay away, no matter how hard she tried.

They settled down, bought a house of their own.
Adopted a dog to make their house a home.
She looks back, thinks how strange it is
that she went through all that, just to get this.

She was told one story by the people she knew
but the older she got, the more that she grew.
Other people's words didn't make her reality
and her broken heart didn't end in tragedy.

ABOUT THE POET

Kristina Adams is the author of 20 novels, 3 books for writers, 1 poetry collection (this one), and too many blog posts to count. She publishes mother/daughter ghost stories as K.C.Adams. When she's not writing, she's playing with her dog or inflicting cooking experiments on her boyfriend.

ACKNOWLEDGEMENTS

Many of the poems in this book I've been sitting on for half my life. Thank you to those who've encouraged me over the years to share my poetry.

Thanks to the ASers for supporting my poetry when I was a teenager. Your encouragement really meant a lot to me.

Thanks to my old poetry class, for encouraging me to experiment and express my voice. I'll always value those classes and the things I learned. And I appreciate everyone from the MA insisting I read as well as host the anthology launch event back in 2014. It helped grow my confidence performing my own work and I don't think I'd have gotten to this point if it hadn't been for that.

Thank you to Alexa for helping me figure out the final poem this book needed. All it took was for you to connect the dots floating in my head and BOOM. Magic. Your faith in me, and your ability to make sense of my half-formed ideas is invaluable and I can't thank you enough (but will try).

Thanks to Chelle for your thoughts and support on my poems, and your insights into trauma and the impact that it can have. I hope you don't mind when I continue to pick your brains for the upcoming *Afterlife Calls* books.

Thanks to Charlotte for listening and supporting. You're such a great friend and I really value you.

Thanks to Millie, for being my emotional support westie. You give me confidence to try new things, a new perspective on life, and can be a great nurse when you need to be. (An aggressively affectionate one, but that's why we love you.)

Thanks to Carl for being my soulmate. For inspiring many of these poems and saving me from myself in ways I didn't know I needed.

And thank you to the people who gave me something to write about.

ALSO BY KRISTINA ADAMS

Nonfiction
How to Write Believable Characters
Writing Myths
Productivity for Writers

Poetry
Revenge of the Redhead

What Happens in Hollywood Universe

What Happens in…
What Happens in New York
What Happens in London
Return to New York
What Happens in Barcelona
What Happens in Paphos

Hollywood Gossip
Hollywood Gossip
Hollywood Parents
Hollywood Drama
Hollywood Destiny
Hollywood Heartbreak
Hollywood Romance

Standalones
    Behind the Spotlight
    Hollywood Nightmare

Boxsets
    Welcome to the Spotlight
    What Happens in… books 1 and 2
    What Happens in… books 3 - 5
    What Happens in… the Complete Collection
    Hollywood Gossip books 1 - 3

Afterlife Calls (as K.C. Adams)
    The Ghost Hunter's Haunting
    The Ghost's Call
    The Mummy's Curse
    The Necromancer's Secret
    The Witch's Sacrifice
    The Mean Girl's Murder
    The Poltergeist's Ship
    The Dead Man's Blood